You Can
Call It
Beautiful

You Can Call It Beautiful

Debra Elisa

MoonPath Press

Poetry
ISBN 978-1-936657-79-7

Cover art: *Le vainqueur* (*The Winner*), etching, 1968
by Graciela Rodo Boulanger

Author photo: Ludger Wöhrmann

Book design: Tonya Namura, using
Gentium Book Basic (text) and Rainer (display)

*Please note: These poems offer poetic truth and make no claims to
biography or accuracy of any other kind. Although some of the
poems reflect moments in history and family life, this collection
is not memoir, and any reference to moments in time or
place are not fit for historical record.*

MoonPath Press, an imprint of Concrete Wolf Poetry Series,
is dedicated to publishing the finest poets
living in the U.S. Pacific Northwest.

MoonPath Press
PO Box 445
Tillamook, OR 97141

MoonPathPress@gmail.com

http://MoonPathPress.com

In Memory of Antje Elisabeth Kaiser,
artist and my mother,
October 29, 1943-December 3, 1996

&

for Ludger

TABLE OF CONTENTS

III. Spirit Rise

IV. Thanks

No one can tell you what to create. . . Just think of the
tree and all of its hard work before you start, he says.
It gave its life for this basket. . . you know your responsibility.
Make something beautiful in return.

—Robin Wall Kimmerer, *Braiding Sweetgrass*

You Can Call It Beautiful

1.
The Way You Move
In The World

We feel like separate water droplets,
But we are also ocean.
—Jane Hirshfield

WE CARRY A PINCH OF SALT

after Lisel Mueller

We carry a pinch behind each word
wilt of Flower
test of mercy
an echo.

We carry a pinch of Salt behind each eyeball
when we remember the words
a book on the table
when I see the Water   the glass
fly across the room.

We carry the pinch though expect
to sit side-by-side sipping Coffee
in the Morning.

I say it's like the sound of a chainsaw.
It's only a toothbrush.

The pinch of longing and doubt.
The pinch of how many words
equal the truth   how many truths
          need to be spoken.

I carry the pinch of *please*
and *don't* and *why?*   Why does the car
pull out in front of me only to stop
and park at the corner?   The pinch
provides umami.
          The pinch is dissolving.

SOMETHING ABOUT THE SEA

after Jay Hopler

There was something of the Sea about it
the way she walked away expecting the Tide
would bring her back the Sea Urchins
Jelly Fish Whales farther out at least
I hoped they'd stay deep and safe
not like the 40-foot Sperm Whale
washed up and fodder
along the Oregon coast
hit by a ship gashed
and she walks away and tells me
I am *irrational.   You are irrational*
she repeats and refuses
when I suggest we start again
this conversation gone awry
Waves tumbling me under
but I swim and breathe
as my arms crawl and reach
back onto Shore and I can't help
my cries of anguish at the sight
of so many broken Sand Dollars
and then I feel the Gulls
surround me
inching close on the Sand
and then I hear the Crows
caw-cawing above as if I am theirs
and belong right here
where I lie sprawled under the Sun
frothy Clouds moving fast
across this moody Sky.

THE WAY YOU MOVE IN THE WORLD

For a long time   I'd ask questions such as
    What is a soul?

    Who created these Trees?
How did Mountains form and human beings

spawn such story?
as if ever it can be explained.

Still   I love the tales   and wonder
about happiness: How in this World

does one find contentment?
What leads a marriage to not only last

but continue to nourish the Earth
fragrance the Air   offer words

that stir
                        what's best in others?

I walk away from certainty
yet tell myself to notice when shoulders

grow tight   a pain in my chest throbs
and when and how it dissolves.

Some will tell you how they live but simply
    can't understand the way you move in this World.

    Notice the Hummingbird as she builds
        her Nest again on your front porch.

Send cookies to the boy off to college last month.
    Simmer a pot of minestrone

        for a newly widowed neighbor.
            Shovel a trench

and take refuge in the Rain that no longer
seeps into your brother-in-law's basement.

    Delight in your mind
        as the boy unwraps

            the box of snicker-doodles   laughter
    as he and his roommates reach for more

                but don't expect a thank you.

Bow and be grateful
    when someone happens to say

        That's just what I needed.

WONDER & TRUTH

I would follow our brother and his buddies into the Woods
where we lived on the edge of houses

children and Dogs barking.   He would roam
with those boys   and I adored them all   feared

        nothing.   When they chased me
I'd spy from the great Oak   climb thick Branches

watch them capture Frogs from Puddles
toss Pebbles into Ants piled high.

                    This girl with braids
            chased those boys

as they prepped
for their next big trip to the Pond   still too young

to know friendship a clear glass jar
        able to hold   all the pickles

            then shards

        flesh and Blood
    in an instance.

Later
in the Evening   we'd fling frisbees

across the Meadow
back and forth

            just for the pleasure.

PRIMAL

I remember when I struggled for words
to speak   emptied fistfuls of pens

etched in notebooks   believing   myself obliged
to light sparks never known to Sky

when I thought writing a story
meant making it all up fresh and alone

song whittled onto walls of magic Caves
whispered up Maples

Orange Blossom   Peacock
until one Spring Morning

we sat hours beneath unfurling Leaves
until heat unleashed their hesitation

guided them as green
protectors

alongside Creek's trickle
no pen in hand

as we wove plot and crayoned
characters that might dissolve

or be embellished.   And   we listened
    as much as we spoke

            comma and tangent
        cracked open endings:

Buck Moon   Sturgeon   Harvest Moon   Hunters

WHAT WE TEACH EACH OTHER TO NOTICE

Under Rocks Crabs scamper
grays and browns of the Beach

hiding   or just living
    in their way

    but sometimes a Green Back
        catches the young boy's

                curiosity.   He holds this Life
            between forefinger and thumb

tosses the masterpiece
    World's Tiniest Scavenger

    into the Tide
        giggling

            as he runs.

                How does it feel to live
                    safe under a Rock

        then tossed toward Sky?

Is friendship broken?

WINTER STORM

Outside the French doors
a Yellow Finch flutters to the feeder

pecks at Seed-offerings
in Wind's whorl

Branches falling from Doug Fir above
as he is joined

by Bird-brothers and sisters
packing in nutrients

to keep bodies robust
as this Winter Storm brews

toward an unknown crescendo
Icy-Rains and I am nudged

cheeks taunt and grinning
witness to Junko   Swallow

and a Grey Squirrel now swings
on the pole   hangs on wire

and tries as she might
tumbling acrobat to raid this farm

that no longer welcomes her weight
and a part of me roots for her success

to crack the code I've created
though she is a winner-takes-all sort

and will leave not a crumb
for others to savor or devour.

FROM OUR FRONT PORCH

for Adelaide Gonzalez

The sound of two sisters' words whistle
onto this sidewalk they've known

since they were teens in a hurry
waltz and Betty Davis

long before babies snuggled tight
into their bosoms

then grandchildren bounced
grabbing toys from a barrel

each wrapped and waiting.
Friends nearby have come and gone

north to Canada or into foreclosure.
Decades ago their daddy made the purchase.

Did he see these Trees planted
giant Norfolk Maple that now shade his girls?

Did he watch for boys   rebuke catcalls
from a roost on his own front porch

pray for safety and grace?   I sit with my pages
swinging bench   Mutt sprawled

on her own worn woven matt
anxious for her next chance   to romp and play

as the sisters laugh   dropping hands
as they open a car door

elegance in this slow dance
                        toward Dusk.

COUNTING PALM TREES

Siquijor, Philippines

I watch women at the tienda pass neighbors
eyes to Sand   meet farmers who live next door

to each other
their wives walk silent   Water buckets balanced

cousins hardly knowing cousins
except for when one had been too drunk

or whose fault it was   passing Day and Night
sometimes at the cockfight.

From my window   house on stilts   I watch
as the rich brother enters the hut next-door

arrived from Mindanao   an Island further south
in this Land of Typhoons   after their mother's fall.

He and his brothers spar for their fair share of copra:
one lame from stumbles long ago

another worn from digging Clay roads
and the rich one admired for his wit and cleverness.

                    The villagers avoid his eyes
as he hoists a bag of Rice and a Goat onto the boat

which will sail him across the Sea.
They do not tell him of the Land's vengeance

or how ghosts will come   no warning
will follow him home to his Island

as my ghosts
                    have followed me

WHO MAKES THESE CHANGES?

after Rumi

This cup stays full now   hot here   burning through
until my love sits again near   sips it dry.

Once a week we walk the Dog along this trail nearby
thick with Needles   fallen Leaves   us   this path
        breath dry.

He toils clearing Branches   Berry Bramble   gone wild
        for the Mountain view   searches   for Seed to dry.

We pull back covers   look out from this window
Snow fall   Cascade Peak gone   Winter Sky.

        If I lift the pot from the Fire fast
    less Water steams away.

Each Drop   alert   bound   under shared Sky
        from this cup   we dream through Night

breath long
            until there is no Light.

18

THE GECKO & THE LEAF

We wondered together
sitting high on a perch

Ocean or Forest?

If only one
where would you go
to escape heart-chill
 and ache

replenish joy
or reinvent in a crusty old Cave
        desirous tingles
                enormous vision?

Together we would run
into a circle of Cedar
release the other's grip
   and each turn to a Leaf
       until we spotted a Squirrel   Gold Finch   or Gecko.

Some Day we'd meet again on a Shore
   perhaps long beyond travels
       Taj Mahal   Odessa   The Great Wall of China

and meander
trip-trop and *bing-bop*
sharing tangles
   prickly and unkempt
       now with the words

that could have brought us together
long ago if only
we had not dreamt most

of losing ourselves
to the Moon.

ODE TO ONWARD

I saw it all. Saw the Otter
tumble and turn on the Pond
the saxophone boasting the blues
Bees singing into the Primrose
and Daffodil   the ecstasy of forces
buzzing and breaking
babies bawling and daddies
giggled. It takes one
to know one. I heard the Thunder
the Camel climbing onto the Tiger's
back   the Cat's purr—so glad
for the company.
It's what I thought.
The lone Wolf   long slender legs
his narrow chest careens
through the Forest
seeking his prey.
I can't blame him either
when he plucks a Sheep
from the herd.
Have you ever been hungry?
And there are Rats in my neighbor's
basement   dead in the traps
and we know Rats can grow angry.
They can see what is happening.
They don't care who pays
the mortgage.
And thank you for Spring.
These Days growing longer
and lighter.   Nothing in my backyard
is created or destroyed
but how it changes.
Tulips will soon purple and white.
Bok Choy will feed us.

The Finches and Juncos will find enough
food elsewhere
and no longer visit.

DEAR FRIEND

You write often of   Trees   Dogs   Birds
she says   and I feel disappointed   because I wish

her to tell me   *You challenge us to consider justice*
and love in all sorts of ways.

Does she remember how the Hummingbird has nested
on our front porch three years running

though this Winter Luca—I call her—raised only one Chick
and the solo babe flew much sooner

from her cradle without a sibling to keep her warm
so the mother was set free

no more food-service delivery
all duties done   by mid-March.

And I wonder   does she feel anguish or joy?
Will she go on to build another Nest

on someone else's front porch
or a Branch in the Cedar in our side yard

and what does my friend find here
besides more domestic Bird-wonder

when protesting the scarring of our Earth
—swaths of Evergreens plowed down for profit

bald Hills for miles as I drive north along I-5—
must be questioned.

I should be persuading my reader
to root for the threatened Western Snowy Plover

to see value in protecting the Columbian White-Tailed Deer
from extinction   how they matter—Loggerhead Sea Turtle

Canada Lynx   Marbled Murrelet   Northern Spotted Owl
the Yellow-Billed Cuckoo   Malone Jumping Slug.

II.
Boy On Bicycle

"The city's innumerable lights
turning on and off remind us
we are born to arrive
as we are born to leave."
—Dunya Mikhail
from *In Her Feminine Sign*

LEARNING THE RULES

for Veronica, Quetzaltenango, Guatemala,
a Spanish Teacher

Arrodillarse
"to kneel"
was once reflexivo
(what you do to yourself)
Pupusas Elote Tacos Rellenitos
until these past years
when soldiers collected
Corn Seed   pointed rifles
men and women
onto their knees
praying for
un milagro
to save them
for their children
who will roam
streets of Crows
no one to hold
their hands
the young
roaming streets of Blood
learning by finding
and taking
smoke swarming
not to read or count or love
but to survive
by Night
by Day avoiding
those who want
to force them
onto their knees

GRIEF MY GRANDMA KNEW

for Anna Forniglia 1914-1998

If only I had known the boy would leap
   one last time from the dock that Day
     his fifteen-year-old spirit   buoyant verve
would ignore my call as our younger brother
   tugged and I pointed
     toward the road above
        Affrettarsi!!   Adiamo!

Only seventeen—a Coal miner's daughter
picnic of garden Tomatoes—and he did adore me
protested when our mother hacked me
a dirty house
simmered sauce too sweet
until that Day when his budding manhood
fists beating on a bearded chest
   took the dive   laughing   merry
     though never to emerge
        and kiss mine   or any other's cheek again.

Our she-Wolf scorned me more
after that Day—my face reminder
               of all she'd lost.

No more hours cooled me in the Lake
   blitz of fear
   Blood and Air
     as if I'd pushed him
   and did not mourn first

when his body refused to breathe again
and I knew how much would never be
and sometimes forgot *it was not me*

though I weep—*Lo amo ancora*
                            and still   his love.

THAT DAY

What if we joined our sorrows?
What if that is Joy?
      —Ross Gay

The thing they never talked about
over spaghetti dinner or pork chops was John

the man who could've been my favorite
who came from Georgia—his thick drawl

shiny glasses   his own two kids and wife
still near Swamp.   He lived downstairs in a room

built especially for him.   Over those months
he told stories   held my hand as I crossed the street

shot games of pool
in that dark-paneled room

beers in hand as laughter nourished
that split-level house until one Winter Day

the garage door flung open
this little girl home early   lunchbox swinging

fell onto her knees   tears and howls
as someone ran into the roaring

turned the key to off
her Dog upstairs—all Mom's Cats

including the Persian
Dad brought home just last week

    dead like John   lying
face-up   on the hood   of that blue   Chevrolet.

A CONVERSATION SHE WANTED TO HAVE

Stories she learned as a child:
gas chambers   Cattle cars
soldiers marching
orders followed
                    feel too near her front door now.

Don't ask about the war   her mother warned
          it will upset her.

The girl watched in seventh grade
films with bodies tossed
millions lined with arms held high
voices stark in unison.

Their teacher said people believed
this tyrant would relieve their hunger
so they could have more
to feed their children.

Don't ask about the war   her father warned
          it will upset her.

The tyrant led them deeper
into dungeons where some would light the match
others eat Fire   all from want
          of mine over yours.

Though she can't know what her grandma would have said
how her heart sank or revved
she imagines an old woman scrubbing floors for strangers
a child eating scraps   cross-legged on shined tile

and wishes she would have asked
her grandma to tell her stories
over and over again

  and imagines how these stories
        might keep the tyrant away.

IN THE HOSPITAL ROOM

My thin drugged smile asks
when will they let me out of here?

I am gaunt and shrinking
tube and wire   heartbeat's rhythm

for all to see. You ask
about my childhood home

to change the subject
and I can see my grandma still

and wish her here with me now
plump fingers holding mine along Rhine walks.

She stuffs coin into my palms
and I run fast through ruins

to fetch bread and she later braids
my hair into silken Puppy-Dog ears

and tells me how she never liked *der Führer*
warned her children to stay away.

Those foggy Mornings.
The fence grown tall.

The rotting Birch.
Without her   I say again

I would not have survived.
   Children just have to figure it out for themselves

she would tell me even then.
Children   they have to figure it out for themselves

I say to you now as you adjust my pillow
and I close my eyes.

THE OXYGEN MAN

Our mother whispers
from the blue couch:

Tell them to speak up normal
loud as usual

or I feel in the way
I'll go away.

She gasps for breath
as threats pulse through me.

I walk into a filled
fluorescent kitchen

tell them they must talk
    as usual.

Don't act like Mom's sick
or she'll go away.

The tank arrives.
A man's voice bellows

his laughter hearty
as he strings tubing

down long hallways
shows our mother

how to point plastic
up her nostrils:

*This can change
the rest of her Life*

he tells us.
Oxygen is not a drug

he assures her.

OIL & WATER

scented fingernails
reached for those brushes

splotches of turpentine
faded into your red smock

before you wandered
through other medians

more lucid & light
paths more—and less

forgiving
    colors that bleed

years later i promise to make order
to catalogue acrylics

charcoaled canvass   pastel
          twisted wires

    you would leave behind

i tell you they will not be lost
yet sometimes the cost

of keeping a promise
to the past

          means more loss

some of these oldest oils
hang on my walls

alongside sketched faces
bold bodies you drew.

CEDAR OF LEBANON

It was after planting the Cedar of Lebanon
in your honor that dusky Day
edge of a clearing
Fir and Alder

 the bench was built
  & Branches grew wide.

You had arrived from the other side of an Ocean
into a World of golden school buses.

The Cedar grew tall
yet gasped from bleeding

 as Sap oozed where a Goat had chewed through Bark:

  He did not know
   we'd made you holy.

Limbs in the Wind whispered
 healing for this World you'd loved

   though longed to leave

 & prayer for the Goats

 who graze like gangsters
  gouging as wild men

   who know not what they harm.

BUOYANT NO MORE

The daughter waits and would like
to thank the Dog

offer milk bones and roasted Chicken
wrap him warm and sing an aria

in his favorite octave
before strangers carry him away.

But she has slid down that slide
into the far away

imagines now how he frolics
fresh leash   loose collar

laughing children playing tag
and then a gentle grooming.

And so she howls   as he had howled
in disbelief   ears drooped

the Day she wacked   her clarinet
on her bare knee   and collapsed

onto the broken woodwind
unable to repair or hide the splinters.

In her mind she pulls him close
as they await a verdict

imagines
no one taken away

and regards him
like a kind brother

who kept her buoyant.

THE ANGEL BELL

I keep the angel bell
and a vase you brought
from a local thrift shop
one red earring from years ago.

You had called from the station.
We piled pillows   tossed rugs
a mattress onto the plywood
of our unfinished attic.

You and I drove one Day into the city
and a woman hollered and pounded
on the hood of my dented Jetta wagon
Please, please help me!
and you chided   *How could you?*
How can you   leave her?
as I drove away.

We should have insisted
you sleep in our bed.
Soon you couldn't hide
the pain as you climbed the steps.

I should have asked you that Day
to talk with the stranger
on the street   broken and alone
for instruction—what to do
when a lost person
asks you for comfort.

I miss those stories you told
of voices   intruders everywhere.

You worried   we'd become like them
and we knew some of what you said
                              was true.

We sat with you those final hours
and you waited until we had walked away.

BOY ON BICYCLE

after Graciela Rodo Boulanger's
Le vainqueur (The Winner), etching, 1968

One painting
on the living room wall
the boy pedals
grin and play
pastel blues
celadon
was gift to you
then left
to me

when I asked
for this delight to hang
in my own home.

The others—charcoal
and sketch   a single brushstroke
acrylic eyes   another crimson
your creations
beginnings and conversation
we continue.

Your portrait—slight smile
glance to camera—
set on my desk
another on a kitchen shelf.

You left us early

and some stories
you believed
were never
true.

JUST AS WE ARE

for my father

Decades have passed since I sat behind the driver's seat
in that golden station wagon

cigarette smoke as we belted along
with Don McLean—*Bye-bye Miss American Pie*

I drove the Chevy to the levy but the levy was dry. . .
Elvis   The Beatles   talk radio   The Doobie Brothers.

Once you played Glen Campbell with such glee
into our backyard as we weeded the garden

and planted fence posts
until Mr. Gilbert called cursing

because he couldn't sleep
and worked Nights at Boeing.

LPs stood tall in the stereo cabinet.
It's where I discovered Johnny Cash   The Byrds

    The Carpenters.   Did you ever bleed
for the Beach Boys?   Cry out for Willie Nelson?

        Lost words sometimes rise up in me as the radio plays
            Fleetwood Mac   Journey   Dire Straits

        and soon I'm singing lyrics
            I never knew I'd ever known.

ON THE WAY TO KHAJURAHO

on a bus in India

All it takes is a flat tire.
Women and Chickens
unpack from the aisles
and bustle toward home
in their village.

You wave me forward
and we wander as we wait
for diesel fume
to again ferry us
toward sacred gods

pairs and trios
statues with eyes
wide gaze from rooftops
once praised
by those living here
off the Land.

Saris of aubergine   azure   black abayas
weave between us now
as we scuttle
fingers twined
fumbling
   footfall & babble

         chapati at Daybreak   yogurt warm on the spoon
                Ginger   and   Sunrise

         charging again
               this peregrine Land

DEAR READER

The poet wonders at the Heron's chosen isolation
her stance of aloofness so much of her Life

and then how she builds her Nest
mudded weeds woven with stray wire in a Rook

amongst many Wings coming and going.
We might Google for facts   and I wonder

about when humans were more committed
requisite for survival.   Did we prepare together

for Cat's Paw and Swales on the Sea
Tornado on Land—eyes on all children

        when Fire burned?   A ceremony was offered
                  for each Salmon slain.

Today the simple Blackbirds
sit caw-cawing up there in the Hawthorne:

For what might they grieve?
How long does a change of direction

      take for a Flock?   Those Crows do not flee fast
but hang out all Day—cries and dives

        to honor the fallen.

TIME IS NOT A ROCK

Mist will seldom fill a Lake.
Air takes Fire into the fresh

    and eldest—tallest of Cedar
      once perch for an Eagle.

Wind blows Clouds as breath.

                It can feel like
          concrete
  the sorrow.

And—what would that mean?

      To axe a brick   a block?

      One's heart?

I walk up the Wooden stairs.

   In time   the crack.

     Nails rust under Rain.   Mud.

Wood is not Metal.
  Metal holds the Flame.

     Heat feeds the Turtle
in its own secret way

   though the Reptile
requires no Tea or Oats
    to warm her

and can live a Life
as long as a human Bear.

Time is soft

not a furnace
or even River.

III.
Spirit Rise

"This was love:
A string of coincidences
that gathered significance
and became miracles."
—Chimamanda Ngozi Adiche

POLISH ONLY THE PEARLS

after Margaret Atwood

I would like to feel your Wings
Bone of jaw
under Moon-glow.   I would like
to pretend again we have never met
   Bone of your jaw
       tender in my grip

and we linger
mystic-Stone
fresh chapati
  Days when we
              trusted ourselves.

I would like to give you back
the first Pearls
give them back so they can mean
   I promise
     but   please   polish
        only the Pearls   nothing else.

I would like to speak your language
but what I would like more
is to know you would again
   give me access   read to me the pages
         point to the Fruit Bat hanging
            in the Kadam Tree.

I would like to quench   slake   though not in gulps
   Mist   trickle   and   its promise
        canal   Current   Cliff

        and its promise
    Rivulet and Tributary
the power to carve
        and to decay.

IRIDESCENCE

after Galway Kinnell

Though sometimes it is necessary to reteach a thing
its loveliness I thought you knew yours forever   safe

a favored Flower   though we couldn't see the underneath
mycelia strung and winding   Roots ravaged   in need
    of Water

then overdosed.   I'd walk on by   let deadheads
take their own sweet time to fall and reseed the garden.   And
    then

one Day you'd held a gun to your own head
and said always you'd known this an option.

You didn't pull the trigger   and now protect the Doe
with her spotted Fawns   breadcrumbs scattered

for the Goose prancing past
into your Pond—her Gaggle close behind.

ODE TO KIRA

This week our Dog is not to be mimicked
nor studied as pinnacle of serenity
or providence of ease and rest—bowl-to-bowl
trot-to-trot   curled and snoozing after duties done.

This Day she doesn't let me out of sight
lies on a blanket near my feet
as I plug away tap-tapping
a time when she could dominate the couch
downstairs perched and ready to serenade
the postal-delivery woman and warn
of strangers—her chance to bark and bawl.

Something haunts this mixed-breed Mutt
concealed from us mere human beings
who admire her usual way to nap at will.

When an Eagle flies high beyond the Cedar's crest
I wonder what might lead this grand Raptor
to wallow? Does she soar despite loss of Wingtip
or Eggs snatched by a Red-tailed Hawk?

Will our Dog dive again into Silver Lake?
We've seen her strokes
have witnessed her ability
to save herself.

Might she find her way
out from this fear—a phobia
caught in her body?

TANGLED

The news   those words   spoken in calm
at least lacking   that tone of effort

that sound of a trained-to-be-a-broadcaster
hit me   a tank   and I am crying

because I'd expected
more news about *Top Grocery* in Buffalo

and she speaks now of a school in Uvalde Texas
mostly Hispanic

a town near San Antonio.
And yet I drive   the next mile

park   under one of those giant Norfolk Maple
in front of our house

and begin to play the Day's WORDL
on my cell phone.

I suppose it's preparation: Our home will be full of Life.
Dinner will need to simmer.

I'll check on the Plum Tree
its Plum Tree Aphids sucking the new growth Leaves

into withered curls that will never open again
an after-dinner chore

and when I return to see him hanging out
on the couch   I say something like

You don't even care about the Plum Tree
do you?   He looks up

and soon he is in the backyard spraying the too-tall Branches
with soapy water because when I spray them

I get soaked   Water into my arm pits.
I cross over to the Peas growing up a trellis

pluck Slugs who crawl on the Bok Choy
pull weeds competing

with the Cucumber starts
and I am gone

    and I am tangled.

MONASTERY DE ENCARNACION, AVILA

for Maria, neighbor of the Sisters

The nuns sing from behind chapel screens each Morning
choose to sleep on boards only inches off cool tile

speak just one hour each Day
no novel   radio   newspaper to read

    But they know!   says a neighbor.

The first words one nun spoke
while out on a voting Day   *Who is this man   Obama?*

Before choosing   some traveled
    Terezin   Phnom Penh   Kigali

doctors and teachers   nourished children and husbands.
More women add their names to a waiting list Day-by-Day

not crawling on their knees as Teresa of Avila
    orders come   *to rise up*   her call to austerity

Doctor of the Church
  as oath

   coarse habits in August
     no heat in Winter—and Oh!

                How they sing!

and I listen
   knowing they will soon return
     to their silence
       me to my train.

VARANASI WINTER

Missionaries of Charity, Varanasi, India

The Sister calls me to bathe one
shrunken   Bone-thick woman

who sits on a cot
eyes glazed

strands of dark hair strewn.

   She takes my hand
     lips pursed

           hums & pulls me closer.

She wants me to touch her shoulders
sacrum   her fingers Birds' feet

barely covered
    by breath.

I want to please this stranger.

Her chest lifts & falls.   She fingers my muscle
    timid bicep   foreign words   silent prayer

        to hurt no one more.

She might not notice grim lights & the stench

as water drips onto her back
rag circling Bone

                    & she lies back
onto her carriage
    curled

into herself.

HER NAME IS KIMBERLY

Along the Willamette
Dog on leash
I meet a woman
her hands gloved
picking up crusted cans
scraps of cardboard
tossing them into a black plastic garbage bag.

Hello   I say   and thank her.
I'm just doing my part   she says   and soon
points away from the River
tents and clotheslines
to where she lives
over there   near McDonalds   blue tarp.

What do you need?   I ask   fumbling
and she says   *nothing*   until we keep talking
and she says   *a shovel*   *yes*   *that would be helpful.*

I   who will return to my four-square
soak in a tub with Epson Salt
feed gourmet grub
to our Mongrel   feel grateful
this woman
maybe a mother
has given me something to do.

I deliver muffins   a book   pens and tablet
energy bars   bottles of Water   a blanket
        along with the shovel
                        only once.

She worked a job   paid rent and taxes
and I wonder what I would say

if I saw myself   trotting along
Dog on leash   sipping from my shiny green Water bottle.

PLACE OF WATER

for Daisy Viernes, Ponong, Siquijor, Philippines

Where Roots of Mahogony once kept the Land lush
Lizards leaping

Fruit of Mango
free to eat

machines pave motor paths
plant poles for electric light

weave wire along now-barren Slopes
as grown children leave for Manila

to hold glints of chrome
between forefinger and thumb

piecing parts together
so a woman a lot like me

in her own cubicle
Prius zooming down I-5

can know the hour at a glance
while these workers in this city

send money home—asking about the Moon
longing to walk in its shine

after a deluge soaks Rice paddies
clears thick heat.

The once-village-girl dreams of her mother's Mung Beans
    Sibuyas   Malunggay Leaves

        blackened pot over Fire's Flame
            dried Fish

        though a TV now blares
    where once she heard boys serenade

        from the bench outside their open window
            twang of worn guitar strings.

THE DETENTION CENTER

The girl and her mother arrive from Utah
14 hours in the backseat of a dusty Corolla

only to learn it's the wrong Day
    for prisoners M-Z.

Her black-braids swing as she sways
near downtown Tacoma

churchwomen offering brown bags
Tuna Fish and Peanut butter

and the girl wonders if ever
she will again feel her father's warm hand in hers

hear his stories. She will begin fourth grade
next month and in the lunchroom

her young and lonely fingers
will place a Rice ball barely bitten

back into a lunchbox tin
    tummy rumbling

a yearning   such desire to convince
those pointing fingers

to befriend her.
She doesn't yet understand

how learning to spell in any language
or ride a bicycle   is easy   but the art

of untangling a mind
full of webbed beliefs

requires more than practice.

CHASING THE RED KITE

The guys go out camping to Trapper Creek
these early Spring Days
while I stay home
happy to meet with friends

on the front porch nibbling crackers
and cheese as we consider Camellias' bloom
Moonlight   and how   we're not sure anymore
about *fun*   splashes of paint   onto a canvas

              white Tulips in a vase
a photo from last week   the woman walking
      through Snowy Woods
                    not a worry in her heart

able to kneel beside a squished Bird
weep and cover the vessel that was a Life
with fallen Leaves   prayer to Orchid
as she opens   beneath Oak and Pine.

But the woman's Forest now burns.
Her eyes spike.   Words pierce and spark
      bodies dodging blasts   she once knew only
            as television clips.

She rallies for memories of running care-free
      across the Steppe   Wind-blown
chasing a red kite but not always does she want
            to lift herself   to gift herself

                  or remind anyone
      of this wonderful Life
the many Lives she has loved
      but she walks into her small garden

still safe   pulls two Carrots   Wintered over
        tears Leaves from the Red Beets
            to simmer for her children
                and any others

        who will join them that Evening
                            to feast.

"NO" AND OTHER CONSIDERATIONS—
ACCORDING TO MR. CHEN

Pudong, China

1.

Be prompt for a meeting and patient for the bus to leave.

The women massaging feet begin at 9am and return home
    after 11pm.

Don't be surprised if someone flags a taxi but insists it's yours.

Be quick to escape out an elevator.

To hear someone say   *I'm sorry*   notice.

One should avoid allowing her luggage to be locked under a bus.

At the market in Shanghai   offer half price.

On the bus   watch how the old woman leans her body
    into the old man's.

On the boat   notice how two young people snuggle on a bunk.

Don't be surprised at subtle groans.

Remember   you can never know who understands English.

2.

If someone answers "yes" it can mean:

> No.
> I don't know if that's possible.
> I don't know what you said.
> That is a bad idea.
> That may be a very good idea   but it's impossible.
> That's an interesting approach   but not something we do.
> Not now.

Are you crazy?
Dumb foreigner. . .
Do you think I'm an idiot?
Can you change the subject?
I will now change the subject.

3.

The idea for building Three Gorge Dam—the largest hydropower
project ever built—on the Yangtze River, began around 1919.
Millions of people have found new homes—their cities, towns
and villages buried deep under Water still rising
where cargo ships now thrum.

RECOVERY

Today our Sun emerges no longer a gorgeous
dangerous orb of these Wildfire weeks.
Eagle Creek in Flames jumped the River
a state—and the Watershed no longer in peril.
Jays mimic up Copper Beech. Squirrels frisky
in the Walnut and Rats from our neighbor's
Chicken coop storm through brittle Berry Bushes.
We invite the Dog's trot along the Willamette
watch her tumble in the Grass the way she does
every time she meets it not a worry of tents
and cookware strewn or masks removed
or whether we'll return tomorrow or next week
Waves cleansing the Beach or tumbling us under.
We toss a stick as she gallops—and watch the Sky.

CALENDULA SEED

for Julie Welch-Bucceri

Imagine these Seeds into garland crown
golden Flowers strung to celebrate

along the streets of ancient Athens.   "Mary's
Gold" Catholics chime   and you'll see

crimson Blooms sail past pyres to honor
those long gone   hung as sacred

Hindu deities along the Ganges.
    Battlefields welcomed Petals pressed

into oozing wounds to stop Blood
from spilling into Mud   as hope

to aid healing   antiseptic Sunshine
stored in those brief faces.   In German soups

spun into salads of the Middle East
sweet engines of Life grow and detoxify

worn ways.   In the Philippines
they are "boho"   *bad smell*   planted to frighten

Insects from eating Rice and Cassava.
Children sow such Seed as these

you left for me   to sprout toward Light
    to watch golden Petals rise from Dirt.

A BIRTHDAY LUNCH

for Cynthia Irvine

My friend planted Daffodils in front
of her 1911 porch years ago.

She means to stay
through the decades

to watch Bulbs bloom
Apple and Plum

sag on the Branches.
Last month she brought a late-Winter

harvest of Arugula.
Today   four yellow-faced wonders

    set in a copper-cup vase
our centerpiece.

From her home near the park
to mine   she pedaled

    maybe wondering
        what she'd nibble once arrived

breath and tiptoe   glory and Clover
        under our feet

            feeding the Earth.

DEAR MR. PRESIDENT

Is it true you choose where drones will ascend?
Let bombs drop in my name?

Do you fund the latest Stealth Flyer
    rather than tracks for fast trains?

How about schools for poor children
doctors and teachers

      without debt for their efforts?

You must sometimes worry

      one Day they will send drones for us:

      High as Hawks   our children will watch

      awed until these "birds"

        blind us further.

SZYMBORSKA'S GUEST

after Wistala Szymborska

Is it a love poem
she writes to the young artist
who sits nibbling biscuits
no apparent place to go

until the young woman finally scurries off
leaving her silky red-purple scarf

hung pretty
        on the rocking chair

    not worried whether
she may have outstayed her welcome?

The older artist wears the scarf now
as she writes the poem

about a young artist who stands
Giraffe amongst Monkeys

vase of Violets
center in this Warsaw apartment.

SPIRIT RISE

*At the hour of zazen I ate chocolate
instead.*
                    Kathryn Hunt, *"Spirit Fox"*

Instead of joining the sangha for an hour
cross-legged on a cushion   I invite the Dog
out for a walk.

Golden Poppies perk between cracks in the sidewalk.
Red ones wiggle in the Wind.

We don't talk much between crosswalks
though I smile at her dark eyes

locked with mine for permission
before she bounds to the other side.

I guide the Dog   though she'll never understand
how a speck so light   a Poppy Seed

grows and leads me onward: Upright and brilliant

        I see it now   crimson and gold
                    Petals on Fire

                when the Sun has shone enough
                    and I am awake.

IV.
Thanks

"The road going home was pocked with holes,
That home-going road's always full of holes;
Though we slow down, time's wheel still rolls."
—Natasha Trethewey, "Graveyard Blues"

A POEM ABOUT JOY

after Alyssa Axsom's watercolor Trance

You've been through darkness, parts of you removed,
and you've cried on shoulders as your lover died.

But now you see with fresh eyes that long for ease.
You walk your Dog along a steep path and then down

into the Trees—where your feet tread Moss and feel relief.
These eyes have studied, and now don't so readily divide

a sunny Day or when caught under smoke-filled Sky.
You take your brushes wherever you go—watercolor

and pencil—and say to the young and to the old

Can I capture your glow?   Please teach me now.

You've been through darkness, and you knew you couldn't stay.
You try now to mine the Ore of the everyday.

You have known darkness, and you don't know when
it might come as Granite—and so here is where you begin.

PANDEMIC LIFE

In our backyard garden I find little Slug damage
these Days of September though Aphids ravage

Kale and suck juice from Tomato Vines.
I visit the beds and snip tonight's dinner: Zucchini

Chard   tender-inside Cukes   for riata or tzatziki.
My neighbor gifts Cabbage and Bok choy

on the woodblock table next to our front door
and I wonder   will there be time left

to enjoy another Summer meal together
their new baby squirming as we giggle

before Rains return   when the chill sets in
and we retreat   again out of sight

into our shut-door lives?
Last week I asked what she'd learned

from these Pandemic times so far.   I expected her to say
it's hard when your mother can't visit from afar

and still hasn't met her granddaughter face-to-face
the isolation while learning to keep up

with a new Life in the house   but she looks at me
smiles and says it's been a good time

to have a first baby
a perfect time

to learn how to parent
lots of time

to focus without all the people
telling you what you should be doing right.

SUNSET

in memory of Mary Elizabeth Welch

You taught me the art
of opening windows
at just the right hour
closing them again
before heat
swept in.
You chose often
not to offer
opinions
so when your granddaughter needed
someone to listen
she would come to you.
And you reminded me to touch gently
a shoulder
kiss a cheek
before parting ways
that this might be
our final margarita
so casually
quaff and quip
into the Evening
we stroll.

GIFT OF THE PURPLE-SPIKED FLOWER

I was 33 by the time I met an Artichoke
rooted in Dirt.   I'd held Petals

steamed and dipped in Garlic butter
teeth scraping clean their meat   avoiding Thorns.

Along that highway   Mom pulled over
next to the loaded pick-up truck.

These globes arrived just once each year   fireworks
to we three kids who grabbed and snatched

Leaf-by-Leaf until down to the heart
which   surprising to me now   we shared

in equal parts.   On Larch Street
I was 33 when my neighbor led me

into her backyard: On the east side grew
two Plants with spiky purple Blooms

cones and pointy.   I jumped with recognition!
The fun we had laughing as we chomped

our father missing out   how he'd never understand
which left more for us   and what if

we had planted those miracles
in our backyard garden   near Corn and Carrots

Pigs and Cows   tending them each Morning
as we set the Horses free to run?

THE ROCKING CHAIR

for Carolyn Norred

You say this chair is one of your best memories
not its red and blue and golden weave now faded

but when your first boy couldn't sleep for Days
when it took medicine 48 hours

to ease the pain in a child's ear.
His crying would stop only against a warm body.

You had been holding him for two Days
the worn velvet cushion

his hot face against your heart beating
Sunlight's early tease

when the door opened   and your neighbor
your mother-in-law   walked into the room.

She took the boy into her arms so gently
he hardly felt the change of comfort.

You go   she motioned
as tears flowed until you fell asleep

feeling like no human being
could love you more than this.

KEEP THE ROUND DOOR OPEN

with a nod to Rumi

We're back to checking in with the clock
because here is where we live

though that tent at Trapper Creek—the Pond
where I stood free and easy
before my wedding Day—I still visit

the Rugosa Roses
native Nootka   Calendula that spread
    weeds of Sunshine across the World
        wonder and wow
though not without its pause for grief.

Did I mention peaceful?
Did I speak with warmth the neighbor child's name
this feeling of melancholy
as the human being sprouts
through thorny terrain

and the dread I can't ignore
when I hear about teachers fleeing.

Are some awakened by the cry
of a Night Owl—lucid dreams
                midday?

    Don't go back to sleep
      Keep the round door open

though you should wear gloves and a hat
in the chill while listening near the exit

and join in song.

   Join in with your song.

THE CARPENTER

She likes to see herself as Diplomat
Elf amongst those Beavers
    tunneling their way through Amerika.

She likes to be Navigator
Owl in an Oak angled from darkness
    Artist into Light.

She likes to be Translator
Chameleon from Leaf to fallen Log
    Spring green to Winter's icy Sky.

She resists the role of Bus Driver
preferring to act as Postal Servant
delivering Stardust and granting wishes:
    Magic Gold   Silver & Ruby-red.

And always she is Carpenter of the Turbulent
World   flouncy with her Words of Bursting
    Joy (*unless they slice!*)

        Alligator   Jaw breaker

    Kangaroo

        Klondike
      Kubla-Kan
            Erudite

    King Tortoise

       White
        Kitten

Appaloosa
ranging through the Prairie

Great Blue Heron returned
to her Rook.

A EUCALYPTUS BOUQUET

Please do not be alarmed
or disappointed—such common states of mind.

Don't let the Tea go cold or choose your mug
according to a grudge:
> *Not that one!   I'll show her!*

Drum out   swim   novelize   root for Pinecones
to fall   into place

for better Bones
better Blood to flow
not from nose but through veins
and arteries

and when your daughter offers to fly
when the young man arrives
lonely and desperate to learn how to breathe
when his friend will not breathe again

read a poem together
   only when everyone feels ready.

        Read it twice.

Let no one insist your Lentil soup needs more Salt.
Let no one tell you who you are
or that Sweet Potato
      will make it better.

Pedal onward   Dance   Sip from the River

READING POETRY TOGETHER

When a man who says he can't enjoy these broken lines
words splattered onto a page picks up the anthology
from the wobbly pile on the Coffee table and reads a poem
the World changes.   He asks about why the poet mentions
green Grass in Spring—so obvious? I have no definitive
response which is much of the joy of reading together or writing
a poem and wondering *where?—from where did this emerge?*
or knowing *from where* and asking *why?*   And what difference
if we simply read the *New York Times*—rant about who might win
how everything will change if *they* get back in office
and *what if* I had knocked door-to-door at least sent postcards
educating those gone astray to vote for what is *reasonable*?
You hand me the book and I read the poem back to you
and know it won't matter more than this who is elected.

POETRY FOR PEACE

Dear Dad: Do you remember when I gave you the book *One Year to Live* and the next year *The Heart Aroused* because back then I thought you needed my advice?

Dear Dr. Dimant: I imagine in England you grew up reciting Donne and Shelley, Milton, Coleridge and Blake. All of these words and soul-verse made you a damn good surgeon.

Dear Students: When I decided to become an English teacher, I vowed to lead you to fall in love with poetry—to read the sort of vibrant verse I didn't find until much later.

Dear Mom: Isn't it wild that all three of your kids write—and read—poetry (and so did you!)? Maybe it's simply the natural way, like how the Vietnamese soldiers carried poems in their pockets. And you were born in wartime. Dead young men were found with words they had scribbled in their final hours.

Dear Mr. College President: I sent a poem a Day out to "ALL" for *National Poetry Month*. Some people loved it and sent back all sorts of confessions, but mid-month—as you know—the music prof sent me a scolding, *How would you like it if I sent a scroll of music every day to your Inbox?* I apologize for the inconveniences I have caused.

Dear Mr. Music Professor: I would love to find a scroll of music in my inbox. I always meant to take *Music Appreciation*, but it was one of those courses everyone took for the easy grade. Back then I wasn't relaxed enough to let the notes and chords enter me without worry of getting it right. Please push delete if my correspondence offends you.

Dear Kira: You are a Dog with a name that means
Beam of Light. You constantly remind us,
poetry is everywhere!

Praise the daily walks! Celebrate kibble!
Lay down, roll over, and allow someone
to rub your belly!
Thank you & sincerely, . . .

A LIFE'S WORK

The Dog barks outside our back door
    leaps and scratches on glass

      almost a howl.
She knows there's nothing more important

I might do now than to stand
    coffee in hand

  & open the door.
She will waltz by my bare feet

eyes' bright aim
        Snack please?

      I'll bling a smile
pull down her stash of peanut butter biscuits.

     She'll roll over   dive under   shake

with each paw
      and we will laugh.

THANKS

after Yusef Komunyakaa

Thanks for this circle of friends who gather
    in praise of poetry   for stories a pen can tell

for listening and for these ears that ring only on occasion
    to tell me
        Slow Down . . . relinquish

And thank you for those moments when I miss the thereness
    of my mother   Aunt Barbara   Karen
        my grandmothers and John

        who I hardly knew when he left us.   I am grateful
        to have never been forced
to flee a bullet   nor slugged in the face or witness to another
person beaten.

Thank you to the voice that forced me once to grip a man's
arm hard and shake
    until he awoke from a trance—only bruised by the mystery.

    The other man set the Iron tool back onto the hearth
and walked out of the room.

Thank you for forgiveness
for all but seven countries in the World (not mine) that grant
    maternity leave and communities who pay
    every worker a living wage

    for *help* that never shames a woman struggling to feed her
        children
or the man who loses his pension when his company goes
bankrupt or moves to Mars.

Thank you for when clean Water is offered without a price tag

for   *Wonder   Hope   Darkness and Light*

more Flowers than guns.

YOU CAN CALL IT BEAUTIFUL

We sit elevated on cushions
   listen as a teacher tells why

  we need to *practice*
    cross-legged   tall-backed

     breath aware   here & now and notice
       wild mind's dance lung-to-lung   elbow-to-toe

Don't get too full of yourself. . .

      she warns   and I think again
       how I want to see again

          My Life as a Dog
      though so little happens

     as the boy
       searches for answers

        to where he might belong
      until the bell brings me back to zafu

and I wonder of Tomatoes ripe   Cornstalk's debut
  in our backyard beds   Aphids' bliss

         reproduction
            every thirty minutes!

Another phone call with my sister missed   my friends'
homelands Cambodia   Burma
   under siege   Kyiv
         places I need to go before I die

but then remember: No more *you must.*

Go!

Tearing Leaves

hands digging.

NOTES

"Iridescence" begins with the line "Though sometimes it is necessary to reteach a thing its loveliness" from Galway Kinnell's poem, "St. Francis and the Sow."

"A Poem About Joy" responds to Alyssa Axsom's watercolor *Trance*.

"Something About the Sea" begins with a line from Jay Hopler's poem "after the diagnosis: mediation on the origins of 'death's thin melody too (variations on an escalator)' by paul rudy" in his collection, *Still Life*.

"Thanks" responds to Yusef Komunyakaa's poem with the same title.

"We Carry a Pinch of Salt" responds to Lisel Mueller's poem "Love Like Salt."

ACKNOWLEDGEMENTS & GRATITUDE

Thank you to the following journals for first publishing a version of these poems:

Kimera: "What We Teach Each Other to Notice"

Kosmos: "Calendula Seed" and "Spirit Rise"

Mute Note Earthward: "Varanasi Winter"

Oyez: "The Way You Move in the World" and "A Conversation She Wanted to Have"

RavensPerch: "Buoyant No More" and "Boy on Bicycle"

The Salal Review: "Counting Palm Trees" and "Learning the Rules"

The Tacoma Reporter: "The Oxygen Man"

Tattoos on Cedar: "'No' and Other Considerations— According to Mr. Chen"

Voice Catchers: "Sunset" and "Gift of the Purple-Spiked Flower"

Oceans of gratitude to the many teachers, students, friends, poets, and artists of all sorts who have shared your voices, encouragement, and curiosity. You've kept me buoyant, and this collection would not live without your input and support along the years.

Thank you to the William Joiner Center for the Study of Peace and Social Consequences for offering me my first writing workshops on the University of Massachusetts Boston Campus decades ago—and to my friend Julie Welch-Bucceri for getting me there. I appreciate Allen Braden for his early encouragement when we were teaching colleagues, and thanks to Dotti Krist-Sterbick, Connie K Walle,

Michael Magee, the late Jean Musser, and Martin Blackman, along with other Tacoma poets.

Thank you to early teachers Bruce Weigl, Bill Lavendar, Hank Lazer, and Jeanne Lutz. More recently thanks to Jill McCabe Johnson, Gail Folkins, Terrance Hayes, Kim Stafford, and John Brehm. Since reading invites us into the circle of creation, thank you Poetry Pals—a fun bunch of creative friends who gather monthly and talk about a chosen collection of poetry. You are terrific!

Thank you to Penelope Loucas, Carolyn Norred, Alan Rose, Glenna Cook, Cynthia Irvine, Tess Kelley, Anne Sullivan, Sharon Carter, Dianne Avey, Carolyn Peck, Paul Hosea, Yvette Raynham, Peter Wood, Betsy Loncar, Eric Fair-Layman, Cassandra Soden, Kathryn Hunt, Peg Edera, Ester Elizabeth, and Sarah Kinsel—each an artist extraordinaire in their own lives. Thank you also to the Moonlit Poetry Caravan—especially Tola Molotkov and Willa Schneberg. Thanks to Lower Columbia College where I taught and co-hosted Northwest Voices.

Visionary and gracious women Julie Reid, Audy Davidson, Kary Hess, and Mandy Steward kept me afloat through the Pandemic years. Thank you for embracing me.

Special thanks and gratitude to poet, editor, publisher, and creator Lana Hechtman Ayers for your spirit and open welcome. I am humbled by your generosity, your boldness as a writer, and all you offer in our communities that lift so many spirits. Never have I encountered such a close reader who offers me so much to consider. You are a gift. Thank you for your patience!

Thank you also to Tonya Namura for her beautiful cover design and to artist Graciela Rodo Boulanger for permission to use *Le vainqueur* (*The Winner*), etching, 1968.

Thank you to my sister, Michelle Sweem, and brother, Dean Brink, both poets who have encouraged me over the years in their own ways. My father, Terry Brink, gave me my first thesaurus, and my mother, Antje Kaiser—a visual artist and poet—modeled the ability to continue creating no matter the circumstances.

With affection and gratitude I thank my husband, Ludger Wöhrmann, for his patience, love, and willingness to keep me near as we grow together. Thank you for paying the bills, for the many remodels, for maintaining my computer and my car, for bookshelves, warming my hands—and listening. I'm glad I caught that bus.

ABOUT THE AUTHOR

Debra Elisa grew up in the shadow of Mount Rainier and fell in love with the land of the Pacific Northwest though longed to travel and learn how people live on the other side of the world. She studied in Glasgow and lived in the Philippines as a Peace Corp Volunteer. She has sat silent in monasteries, gazed up at birds in a sanctuary, and lived in New England for a half dozen icy winters. She met her husband while traveling in India. Together they rode buses along the Trans-American Highway from Guatemala to Argentina as part of a sabbatical. She now lives in Portland, Oregon, where they grow food in their backyard garden and can go days without driving a car. She leads *Poetry Play* and other creative workshops and offers Somatic Bodywork when not writing, cooking, or wandering in the woods or along coastal beaches. She blogs at www.l-i-t.org Live(s) Inspiring Today and welcomes your visit.

Printed in the USA
CPSIA information can be obtained
at www.ICGtesting.com
LVHW091310230224
772520LV00002B/310